Original title:

Sunlit Ferns

Copyright © 2025 Creative Arts Management OÜ

All rights reserved.

Author: Nash Everly

ISBN HARDBACK: 978-1-80581-931-8

ISBN PAPERBACK: 978-1-80581-458-0

ISBN EBOOK: 978-1-80581-931-8

Ferns Aglow in Morning's Kiss

In the bright dawn, ferns giggle so,
They dance with dew, putting on a show.
Whispers of green, a playful tease,
They sway in rhythm, fluttering with ease.

Beneath the rays, they flaunt their flair,
Tickling the grass, beyond compare.
With every breeze, they poke and prod,
Joking with flowers, it's quite the facade.

Verdure Bathed in Gentle Rays

In verdant shades, they plot their schemes,
Telling tall tales of sunbeam dreams.
Each frond a character, winking bright,
Caught in the glow, what a silly sight!

Ferns in the field play hide and seek,
With cheeky smiles, they playfully peek.
Whirling in laughter, what a delight,
Every shadow chuckles, pure and light.

Light's Tender Touch on Earth

As light tiptoes, the ferns cheer loud,
Daring the sun to join the crowd.
They giggle and wiggle, a comic scene,
Each is a joker, the green routine.

Under the glow, they spin and twirl,
Chasing each other in a leafy swirl.
A banquet of laughter, nature's bowl,
With roots wrapped tight, they rock 'n' roll.

Green Enchantment Beneath the Stars

When night descends, the ferns still play,
Trading the sun for the moon's ballet.
They whisper stories of the day's fun,
Until the dawn brings a new run.

Under the stars, they conjure a jest,
Mocking the shadows, they never rest.
With a flick of a leaf, they share a grin,
In this leafy show, everyone wins!

Illuminated Ferns in Still Waters

Ferns play hide and seek, so sly,
Beneath the shimmer, they wave goodbye.
They giggle softly, twirling in pools,
While frogs take bets on who breaks the rules.

A fish swims by, all puffed with glee,
"Who knew ferns were so full of esprit?"
The rippling laughter echoes in waves,
As dragonflies dance, the spotlight they crave.

The Caress of Light on Leafy Boundaries

Oh leafy green, you jest and tease,
Tickled by shadows, swaying with ease.
The sun pokes fun, behind clouds it hides,
While ferns shout tales of their wild joy rides.

A worm in a hat joins their leafy jest,
"I'm the king of soil," he declares with zest.
The sunbeam chuckles, as ferns take a bow,
"This party's epic, come join us now!"

A Tapestry of Verdant Dreams

In a patchwork quilt, the ferns convene,
Whispering secrets, if you know what I mean.
They pull pranks on leaves, who giggle and sway,
"Oh look, that one's got a leaf-mustache today!"

The creeping vines join in the fun,
"Pluck a leaf, let's see who can run!"
Nature's own jester, with laughter they blend,
In this merry green, the jokes never end.

Beneath the Brightness of Nature's palette

Below the blaze, the ferns play shy,
Like goofy recruits in a leafy tie-dye.
They twirl with a wink, they blink with delight,
While critters cheer on, what a silly sight!

The sun rolls its eyes, says, "Can't you behave?"
But ferns just giggle, and mischief they crave.
"Life's more fun," they cry, "when we dance in the light!"

And with a twinkle, they vanish from sight.

Flourish of Life in Glowing Light

In the garden of giggles, the greens all sway,
Waltzing to whispers of a delightful play.
Frogs in tuxedos hop, feeling quite grand,
While daisies in tutus dance, hand in hand.

Laughter erupts from a nearby stump,
Where a squirrel does somersaults, landing with a thump.
The daisies all cheer, they know it's a show,
As a sunflower joins in, putting on quite a glow.

Colors that Breathe in Harmony

In the meadows of mirth, where colors collide,
A butterfly sneezes, oh what a wild ride!
The purple bellflowers giggle in glee,
While the red poppies roll, feeling so free.

A rainbow parade wobbles down the lane,
Mixing up shades like a painter's fun game.
"Let's prank the sun!" said an orange so bold,
As teasingly it changed into blue and gold.

Ephemeral Rays on Velvety Leaves

Waves of green giggle as shadows poke through,
A caterpillar chuckles, "Just me, trying to chew!"
Leaves whisper secrets, tickling the breeze,
As light drizzles in, like syrup on cheese.

Hopping along, a rabbit tells tales,
Of how he once sailed on the back of a whale.
"Bright streaks of delight, oh what a grand phase,
You should wear a hat, to soak in the rays!"

A Vision of Bright Abundance

The patchwork of smiles in a whimsical field,
Each petal a story, each root a shield.
"Watch out for the shadows!" the daisies exclaim,
As bright little bumbles join in on the game.

With laughter as currency, they trade jokes in the sun,
A clover with style triples the fun.
"Let's have a tea party!" quipped a cheeky chive,
Sipping on sunshine, feeling so alive!

Essence of Light in Lushness

In the forest, ferns dance bright,
Hats made of green, in pure delight.
They laugh at shadows, skip with glee,
Sipping sunshine, oh, what a spree!

A froggy hop, a silly swish,
Ferns raise a toast, 'To every wish!'
With twinkling, giggling fronds, they sing,
A chorus made for the bright spring.

A Shimmer of Growth

Ferns stretch their arms, what a sight,
Reaching for snacks, under warm light.
'Is that a snack? Oh, what a tease!'
A caterpillar munches, aiming to please.

Swaying and swooping, it's quite the show,
Ferns giggle as butterflies start to glow.
In this wild garden, with branches that tease,
Even the bees are having a spree!

Tranquility in Glowing Hues

In the glade where giggles bloom,
Ferns wear smiles, banishing gloom.
Scattered sunlight, a fairy parade,
With pinky toes dipped in water, unafraid.

A rabbit hops, a dance of cheer,
Ferns wave hello, no need to fear.
Oh, the joy of this leafy crew,
Sometimes they'd swear they saw a shoe!

Harmonies of Leaf and Light

Ferns host concerts, leaves in a jam,
A symphony of chirps, a nature slam.
With sunlight weaving through the crowd,
These leafy grooves make laughter loud.

A grasshopper tries to break the mold,
Doing the worm, but feels quite bold.
The ferns roll their eyes, yet can't resist,
Joining together, funk like this!

Nature's Green Hues at Daybreak

A leaf sneezed, the wind took flight,
It tickled grass with sheer delight.
A squirrel danced with such a flair,
Chasing shadows, without a care.

Beetles waltzed on petals bright,
They twirled around in pure daylight.
A bunny giggled, tried to bound,
But tripped on roots, fell to the ground.

The daisies acted quite aloof,
Pretending they were made of poof.
While butterflies played tag on high,
One missed its turn and kissed the sky.

Morning's charm fills every space,
As nature wears a joyful face.
With laughter spliced in every beam,
We find the day is but a dream.

Sunbeams Across a Lush Tapestry

A frog croaked jokes, oh what a spree,
As petals laughed, they teased a bee.
The sun tickled an old oak tree,
Its branches shook, quite merrily.

Mice threw a party, quite absurd,
They served up crumbs, oh how they purred!
The dandelions joined the fun,
Rolling in circles, one by one.

A butterfly stumbled, why oh why?
It landed wrong, not meant to fly.
But cheered by friends, it rose with glee,
Doing the dance of jubilee.

Laughter rings through every glade,
In nature's grand and light parade.
With every ray that warms the ground,
We find the joy that's all around.

Glimmering Spirit of the Woods

A chipmunk juggled acorns with flair,
While squirrels critiqued, declaring it rare.
The trees whispered tales of the day,
While mushrooms giggled, 'Hip-hip-hooray!'

In shadows, a hedgehog spun around,
Kicking up leaves, such fun could be found.
A rabbit munched on a dandelion,
But forgot it was still a tie-dye lion.

A crow cawed, wearing glasses so chic,
Declaring, 'Nature, it's time for a tweak!'
While fireflies burst into a dance,
As if to say, let's take a chance!

Each corner of green wore a bright grin,
As if the day was all meant to spin.
The woods invite all creatures to play,
In giggles and joy, we spend our day.

Secretive Spirals of Green

A snail disco-ed, slow as can be,
Inviting all critters, 'Come dance with me!'
While ivy snickered from her wall,
'The faster you go, the less you'll fall!'

Curly ferns waved as they swayed,
Their spirals told tales of the plans they'd laid.
A curious fox peeked from behind,
As mushrooms whispered, 'You're quite blind!'

With laughter echoing through the trees,
A breeze swirled in, spreading glee.
Each creature shared a chuckling rhyme,
In a world where fun knows no time.

When daylight dances on every stalk,
A burst of joy is what we'll unlock.
So here we twirl, with nature's delight,
In greens that giggle under the light.

Dappled Dreams Beneath the Trees

In the shade, a frog does dance,
With moves that leave all in a trance.
A squirrel giggles, tail in air,
While leaves whisper secrets everywhere.

A caterpillar wears a hat,
Upside down, he thinks he's fat.
The beetles join with great delight,
A disco party, what a sight!

The branches sway in laughter too,
As shadows play a peekaboo.
The wind joins in with gentle sighs,
While sunlight winks from secret skies.

And so the day rolls into fun,
With leafy beats and jokes well spun.
Beneath the trees, a joyful crowd,
Nature's giggles growing loud.

Ferns that Catch the Dawn

As morning breaks, the ferns all cheer,
They sip the dew, then dance with sheer.
One ferns says, 'I'm feeling spry!',
Another quips, 'Oh me, oh my!'

A grasshopper leaps, a jester bold,
He cracks a joke, the ferns unfold.
They shimmy quick, a leafy spree,
With laughter floating, wild and free.

A sunbeam tickles every frond,
Each laugh ignites a hidden bond.
They trade their tales of moonlit nights,
While birds compose their morning rites.

As laughter fades with rising glow,
They whisper secrets, tales to sow.
Ferns in frenzy, a merry throng,
In dawn's warm light, they all belong.

Glowing Grasses in Stillness

The grasses stand, a verdant crew,
With whispers soft, they start their brew.
'Who needs a wave?' one boldly brags,
'Just watch me sway, I'll raise the flags!'

A beetle rolls by, donning shades,
He struts along, in cool charades.
The sun reflects on dewy tips,
As laughter bursts from leafy quips.

One clump is tickled by a breeze,
'Why can't we dance?' says one with ease.
A rustle, giggle, swish and sway,
Nature's jesters at play all day.

As shadows stretch and twilight dims,
The grasses hum their merry hymns.
In stillness found is joy so bright,
Glowing gently in fading light.

Nature's Kaleidoscope of Light

A spin of colors, greens and golds,
Where sunlight dances, fun unfolds.
The flowers chuckle with delight,
As butterflies take their grand flight.

'The day is ours!' the daisies shout,
They twirl and spin without a doubt.
A bumblebee joins with a buzz,
Inviting all to laugh, just because.

The trees sway gently, roots entwined,
While sunbeams play, so intertwined.
Each petal sways with rhythmic flair,
The vibrant joy fills up the air.

With every hue, all nature sings,
A spectacle of playful things.
In laughter's glow, our spirits light,
A wondrous show, pure, fun, and bright.

Glimmers through the Foliage

In the green, a giggle hides,
Little critters find their rides.
A squirrel bounces, takes a leap,
Chasing shadows, dreams to keep.

Dancing leaves in sunlight's game,
Whisper secrets, tease a name.
A cheeky raccoon strikes a pose,
Winks at me, with a nose that glows.

Tall stalks sway, they laugh and play,
Tickling bugs that start to sway.
With every rustle, nature's jest,
Who knew that ferns could laugh, no less?

Among the stalks of leafy cheer,
Jokes abound, and giggles near.
Nature's wit, oh what a sight,
In ferns so bright, laughter takes flight!

Lush Resplendence in Bloom

In a jungle of lush delight,
Frogs in sunglasses, quite the sight.
A butterfly trips on a leaf,
Flies and giggles — disbelief!

Beneath the bright, a worm's parade,
A wiggly dance, a silly charade.
The flowers cringe, but can't resist,
A bloom brings smiles, like this twist.

Dripping color, splashes of fun,
Even the ants join in, on a run.
A picnic planned, though crumbs unfold,
As nature's humor starts to mold.

Adventures sprout in vibrant hues,
Sassy blooms that sing the blues.
Amidst the green, a laugh or two,
Joy in every dew-kissed view.

A Tapestry of Bright Green Dreams

A tapestry of leafy glee,
Aspiring to dance, just like me!
A grasshopper recites a pun,
In a chorus—nature's fun!

Among the fronds, a chameleon grins,
Changing colors, he still wins.
Oh, who knew greens could get so wild?
Playful nature, forever a child.

Flower buds know how to tease,
Tickled by bouncing summer breeze.
They giggle madly, swaying along,
Singing their own silly song.

Underneath this leafy dome,
Every critter feels at home.
In the lush, a joyful spree,
Nature's humor, wild and free!

The Hidden Glow of Nature's Cradle

In nature's cradle, jesters scheme,
A toadstool whispers, "Join my dream!"
Wiggly vines take to the ground,
In every twist, a laugh is found.

A gnome with antics, winks his eye,
Pretends to fish in the butterfly.
The blooms erupt with giggles bright,
Tickling petals in pure delight.

Crickets hold their nightly show,
With cricket jokes, they steal the glow.
They chirp and chatter, what a blast,
As shadows dance beneath the vast.

Twinkling stars, the ferns applaud,
Cheering on the hilarious squad.
In the glow of the night's embrace,
Laughter echoes in this sacred space.

A Stroll through Verdant Luxury

In a lush place where the cooties dance,
 Ferns wear hats, oh what a glance!
 Whispers of wind play a silly tune,
While squirrels giggle under the moon.

A dapper snail with a cane shows pride,
 Jumps on a leaf and takes a slide.
 'What a ride!' he shouts with glee,
While everyone else just sips their tea.

A lizard's doing the moonwalk cool,
 On a damp rock, he's no fool!
 He flips and flops and wears a bow,
While rabbits cheer, 'Go, buddy, go!'

In this green patch where laughter stirs,
 Nature's jokes will always whirs.
Let's skip and bounce, feel the frolic thrum,
 In this lush, luxurious love of fun!

The Dance of Light and Leaf

Fluttering about, a beetle's grand ball,
With petals as gowns, they twirl and sprawl.
Each tiny friend gives a wink and a laugh,
While ants in tuxedos carve out a path.

A big ol' frog with moves so slick,
Catches a fly with a charming flick.
'You're all invited to my soirée!'
With a grin like that, how could they say nay?

The breeze carries jokes from flower to flower,
Tickling the leaves for the next hour.
While a punny vine wraps its pals so tight,
Squeezing with laughter, what a delight!

In this giggle fest, under rays so bright,
Every moment shines, oh what a sight!
With fronds that wiggle, it's a leafy spree,
Join in and dance, it's a laughter decree!

Enchanted Understory

Deep down low where the giggles grow,
Fungi wear shoes, oh what a show!
A hedgehog juggles an acorn or two,
While a wise old owl just hoots, 'Boo-hoo!'

The mushrooms trade tales of the days gone by,
As shadows bounce under a bright blue sky.
A caterpillar croons a silly song,
And all the critters sing along!

Flowers making plans for a comedic skit,
Where bees act out, but forget each bit.
A ladybug giggles and rolls on the ground,
'How can it be, that I've lost my sound?'

In this undergrowth of playful cheer,
Laughter and joy fill the atmosphere.
So tiptoe on in, join the whimsical spree,
Where every heart dances, feeling so free!

Twilight's Caress on Verdant Plains

As dusk turns the sky a playful mix,
Critters plot schemes, oh what silly tricks!
Fireflies come out for a neon dance,
While rabbits try out their best moonlit prance.

The grass tickles toes as they wander near,
While crickets chirp, 'We're the band here, dear!'
A hedgehog just tripped on a shoe left behind,
Squealing with laughter, oh what a find!

A chubby fox wears a hat made of grass,
Chuckling at things that too quickly pass.
'Why did the chicken cross the lane?'
To join the critters in their giggly refrain!

As the sun sinks low and the stars start to peek,
Nature's jesters keep entertaining all week.
So join in the fun, let your laughter reign,
In this twilight caress, hang up your mundane!

Parables of the Forest Floor

In the green circus, leaves delight,
Frogs in top hats, bouncing in flight.
Mushrooms dance to a silent cheer,
Squirrels in tuxedos, oh dear, oh dear!

Twirling round in a leafy dress,
Ladybugs gossip, no need to stress.
A snail with a cane, taking it slow,
Crickets sing tunes for the evening show.

Down by the roots, a raccoon spins,
Telling tall tales of forest sins.
With acorns for jewels, and laughter galore,
Nature's own jesters, forever they soar.

So gather round, in the underbrush,
Where fables grow in a leafy hush.
Each wanderer grins, as they tread once more,
For who knew the woods could jest and roar?

Bright Crescents of Verdure

Wobbling ferns with a comedic flair,
Dancing like they just don't care.
Beetles put on their finest shoes,
Making the petals laugh, not snooze.

Underneath vines, a party unfolds,
Lizards in shades, doing bold molds.
With a wink and a leap, they shimmy and glide,
Tickled by winds on this joyful ride.

Even the roots join this merry spree,
Giggling gently, quite whimsically.
Twisting and turning in the cool shade,
Forest shenanigans never do fade.

Each leaf is a source of hearty jest,
Pooling laughter, nature's best fest.
Amongst this green, so vibrant and bright,
Every creature knows, joy is in sight.

The Quietude of Shimmering Greens

Whispering grasses with secrets to tell,
A sloth in a hammock, it's hard to spell.
While bunnies gossip in the leafy halls,
Gardeners of jest, behind bark's walls.

Crickets wear spectacles, pondering fate,
As ants hold a meeting to contemplate.
With tiny debates and the sun slipping low,
Who knew such thoughts in the forest could flow?

Under soft canopies, a raccoon theorizes,
On ripe fruit and baking, much to his surprises.
While moles dig deep for treasure untold,
With dreams of a bakery, oh, if dreams could hold.

So keep an ear close as shadows decline,
For even in stillness, the forest will shine.
In the quietude where laughter is keen,
Nature's charms blossom, oh how they're seen!

Lush Gleams in the Morning Mist

Morning dew dons a frosty wig,
As creatures wake, then begin to jig.
The shyest mouse with a wink and a nod,
Finds a disco ball, how very odd!

Grasshoppers tap dance on pliable thorns,
Mocking the roses, adorned with scorns.
With petals for hats, and laughter that soars,
The concert unfolds on the woodsy floors.

Glancing back, a turtle quite fast,
Stumbles upon mist that cannot last.
In the midst of whimsy, the fun multiplies,
Amidst giggles and whispers, the sunlight will rise.

So join in this jest, my dear forest friends,
With ferns as the champions, where laughter transcends.
For in every beam, and each playful twist,
Nature's light heartedly draws us in its mist.

Untold Secrets of the Underbrush

In shadows deep where whispers lie,
A critter jokes as leaves drift by.
Ferns giggle at the passing breeze,
Sharing antics of the buzzing bees.

Rooted here, they plot and scheme,
Like nature's kids in a grand daydream.
With laughter wrapped in emerald hues,
They prank the birds, leaving them confused.

Beneath the fronds, a dance unfolds,
A conga line, the ferns are bold!
They frolic low, while secrets hide,
In the lush jungle where mischief abides.

So if you wander where they dwell,
Listen close to their leafy spell.
For all that giggles in green and brown,
Are ferns that laugh without a frown.

The Serenity of Sun-Kissed Leaves

Warm rays bounce on grassy knolls,
While ferns tell tales of silly shoals.
A wiggle here, a wiggle there,
Ferns gossip 'bout a squirrel's lost hair.

With every swish, they crack a joke,
Under the sun, their laughter spoke.
When shadows play hide and seek,
The ferns all giggle, oh so meek!

They prance around in whimsical glee,
In dainty dance, all carefree.
The sun's embrace, a warm delight,
As ferns debunk the myths of night.

So roam where they bask in golden cheer,
Embrace the quirks that nature steers.
For in each leaf, a story we find,
Of joy and laughter, nature's kind.

Hues of Nature's Gentle Aura

A palette bright in colors strange,
As fronds arrange for a playful change.
They shimmer bright, a vibrant tease,
Telling stories on a gentle breeze.

Every hue has a silly name,
Those ferns are in the laughter game.
Chartreuse chortles, emeralds grin,
While sapphire fronds dance with a spin.

In cozy patches, they congregate,
Swapping tales till it's getting late.
How a raindrop caused a fern's wild pirouette,
And made a snail feel quite upset!

With roots in laughter, they bond with flair,
Creating joy in the cool, sweet air.
So when you stroll amidst this scene,
Remember their antics—funny and green!

Fern Fronds in the Morning Glow

Morning light brings a vibrant show,
Where ferns lay low, basking in the glow.
They shake off dew like a chuckling friend,
Starting the day with laughter to lend.

A flash of green, a burst of cheer,
To tickle each bug that happens near.
Whiskers twirled in a playful swoon,
As fronds dance lightly, hum a tune.

In the crisp air, a joke takes flight,
Tickling thoughts until they're light.
Those fronds, you'd think, are in a play,
Turning the dawn into a cabaret!

So as you greet this mirthful morn,
Join the laughter where ferns are born.
For in their world of leafy cheer,
Every moment is sweet and clear.

The Subtle Glow of Nature's Craft

In the woods where giggles creep,
Green fingers tickle roots so deep.
Each leaf a joker, quite a tease,
Spreading laughter on the breeze.

With a wink, the sunlight dances,
Making merry, taking chances.
Ferns in frolic, hearts aglow,
Who knew plants had such a show?

Nature's brush with amusing flair,
Creates a scene beyond compare.
Paints the ground with vibrant cheer,
Every step a chuckle near.

Whispers from the green brigade,
Jokes exchanged in leafy shade.
They conspire with the breeze's sigh,
To make the shyest critters fly.

Glistening Ferns Amidst the Shadows

In the shadows where the ferns reside,
Lurks a giggle, can't hide inside.
Rustling leaves, a sneaky play,
Plays peek-a-boo, come what may.

Dew drops slipping from their tips,
Chasing down mischievous quips.
They gather giggles like confetti,
With a bounce as light and ready.

Ferns in a whisper, oh so sly,
Plant comedians on the sly.
With puns that grow on emerald stems,
Sprouting laughter instead of gems.

Light streams in with a giggling shout,
Tickling brown spots without a doubt.
Nature's humor, leafy and spry,
Making even stumps crack a smile wide.

The Heartbeat of Shining Greens

In the heart of every fern there lies,
A silly spirit in disguise.
They wave their fronds, say, 'Join the fun!'
Under watchful gaze of the sun.

Twirling 'round as if to say,
Life's a party, come what may!
With every rustle, a joke unfolds,
Nature's punchline, bold yet old.

Ferns slap high-fives with bumblebees,
And joke with breezes through the trees.
They shimmy and sway, never miss,
In their world, it's a leafy bliss.

The heartbeat's rhythm is a chuckle,
Each thump a hint of leafy shuffle.
A dance of joy in emerald sheen,
Where every leaf is a jester keen.

Dreaming in a Sea of Ferns

Where dreams float softly in the air,
Ferns are the pillows, everywhere.
They whisper tales of funny dreams,
With giggles hiding in their seams.

Dancing shadows take a breather,
While the ferns spin tales that tease her.
In this green sea, laughter dives,
Tickling fancies, brightening lives.

Sprouting stories on emerald beds,
Jesters' crowns upon their heads.
Floating in a comic stream,
Nature's pun on a sunny beam.

When night falls soft, and dreams take flight,
Ferns giggle softly, a sheer delight.
In a world of wonder, smiles emerge,
As sleepy heads in the breezes surge.

The Bright Caress of Forest Spirits

In the forest where giggles play,
Foliage dances in a quirky sway,
Tree trunks wiggle, trying to tease,
Even the squirrels laugh with ease.

Beams of laughter filter down,
While mushrooms wear a funny crown,
A rabbit hops in awkward spins,
Telling tales of woodland sins.

The bushes rustle with glee and fright,
As shadows wiggle, taking flight,
A raccoon plays a jester's role,
Stealing snacks from the ants' whole bowl.

With every breeze, a chuckle ignites,
Nature's jesters in leafy tights,
In this forest, full of charms,
Finding joy in nature's arms.

Radiant Veils of the Woodland

Amid the woods where sunlight pranks,
Mushrooms glow like cheerful tanks,
Ferns wave their leafy hands,
In secret laughter, the forest stands.

Grasshopper hops with flair so bright,
His dance a spectacle of pure delight,
The flowers giggle, their colors grand,
While bees make jokes that are quite unplanned.

The whispers of leaves are mischief-made,
As chipmunks in a wild charade,
Through radiant veils, the critters play,
In a woodland ballet, bright and gay.

Every inch alive with jest,
Where daylight shines upon their quest,
In this stage of leafy fun,
The woodland's laughter has just begun.

Lattice of Shadows and Sun

In a patch where shadows twirl,
Dancing leaves are in a whirl,
The sun gives chase to every prank,
While critters plot in a leafy bank.

Twisted vines and wiggly roots,
Shady figures play the flutes,
A toad croaks out a comedy,
Pouring laughter like a melody.

The latticework of light and dark,
Is painted with a cheeky spark,
A fox tiptoes, then bursts in glee,
As shadows spread like a wild jubilee.

With a wink, the sun starts to tease,
Inviting fun amongst the trees,
In this vivid patch of terrain,
Laughter echoes again and again.

Bright Embrace in the Greening Air

Beneath the boughs where giggles spin,
Jokes are hidden, always begin,
A parrot squawks a silly rhyme,
As sunlight dances, marking time.

Frogs leap in synchronized cheer,
Splashes of laughter, oh so near,
While mossy cushions cradle the jest,
In this haven, the heart's at rest.

A sunbeam tickles the old oak's nose,
And down it chuckles, as everyone knows,
The ferns hold secrets, playful and bold,
In this lively tale, winter feels cold.

With each breeze, laughter takes flight,
In the greening air, spirits unite,
As nature's jesters join in the fray,
Inviting all to join in the play.

Garden of the Glancing Sun

In the garden where giggles bloom,
Frogs wear hats that chase the gloom.
The daisies dance in silly prance,
As butterflies join in the chance.

A gnome takes a nap on a mushroom cap,
While squirrels plot a sneaky trap.
The daisies gossip, 'Who's that guy?'
Oh, it's just the scarecrow saying hi!

A pesky bee buzzes with flair,
It thinks it's crowned the garden's heir.
The pansies laugh, their petals bright,
As they attend the pollen fight.

A windy gust sends hats a-flying,
And garden guests start squealing, crying.
But in the air, joy is spun,
In this garden of the glancing sun.

Cresting Waves of Green

Waves of green roll in with a cheer,
Merry mushrooms sway, lend an ear.
A snail in shades glides with style,
As grasshoppers jump with a laugh and a smile.

An ant in sunglasses struts on a leaf,
Holding playtime close, no room for grief.
While the crickets compose a funny song,
Each note a giggle that could last long!

Twirling twigs in their dance-like squats,
Dodging doodlebugs and silly spots.
While lizards break out in tap dance shows,
Underneath the converse of leafy bows.

With every sway and twist that they make,
The joys of green surely won't break.
Where laughter swells in nature's scene,
In these cresting waves of green.

Glints in the Mysterious Underbrush

In the underbrush where shadows play,
Funny creatures are at sway.
A raccoon wearing a bowler hat,
Sneaks away with a shiny spat!

The bushes chuckle, holding their breath,
As a mole recounts his near-death.
A squirrel with sass scampers about,
As the flowers giggle, no reason to pout.

A hedgehog dons a tutu so pink,
Makes the crickets stop and rethink.
They all gather for a movie night,
Underneath stars that shine so bright!

Glints of laughter scatter around,
In this underbrush, joy is found.
Nature's fun in a wild rush,
Crawling and laughing, a crazy hush.

Texture of Light on Soft Surfaces

With textures glowing in a playful hue,
A rabbit juggles, oh what to do!
The light plays tricks on fluffy hay,
While bunnies bounce in a merry ballet.

Sunbeams tickle every soft spot,
As chipmunks debate who's got the best plot.
A ladybug holds a comedy show,
Telling giggles to those who slow.

The petals shimmer, a stage so bright,
Where ladybugs dance, what a delight!
And on the grass, laughter unspools,
As bees and insects break all the rules.

In this scrapbook of light and glee,
The textures of joy for all to see.
With each giggle, laughter we brace,
In the fun-loving soft surface space.

Spring's Breath within the Shade

In the garden, a squirrel walks by,
Wearing a hat made of leaves, oh my!
He trips on a twig, does a little spin,
And pretends he meant it, like 'Look at my win!'

The bees buzz around in a wild, loud tune,
Dancing like they're at a costume party in June.
A butterfly flutters, in shades of bright blue,
Asking a snail if he's got a clue.

A flower sneezes, pollen flies high,
A ladybug laughs, gives it a try.
She rolls on the ground, comes up with a smile,
Saying, 'That's the best sneeze, stay a while!'

The sun peeks through with a cheeky grin,
As if to say, 'Let the fun begin!'
Nature's a show, and we're all in play,
So come join the laughter, and dance the day away!

Emerald Dreams in the Sunshine

In the bright patch where the orchids bloom,
A bunny hops in a wizard's costume.
He waves his wand, or at least he pretends,
While dreaming of carrots as his magic blends.

A leaf pirouettes, a gentle twirl,
In a daring dance, oh what a whirl!
The grass giggles softly, a playful tease,
As ants march in line, proud as you please.

A kite flies high, tangled in vines,
Dogs chase their tails, making silly lines.
A tree listens close, trying not to laugh,
As it watches the madness on this sunny path.

Dandelions pop, like confetti so bright,
In a spontaneous party, what pure delight!
The birds join in, singing silly rhymes,
While squirrels keep score of the best of times!

Nature's Canvas of Light and Leaf

A canvas draped in shades of green,
Where frogs play hopscotch, a sight to be seen!
With sticks for chalk and mud for the board,
The frogs giggle loudly at their own crazy score.

A wise old owl sits shaking his head,
Watching the chaos, amused in his spread.
He shouts, 'Hey now, you kids, take it slow!
This is not a race, let your fun really flow!'

A squirrel with sunglasses struts like a star,
Sipping on raindrops, feeling bizarre.
He flips his tail as a dance move so fine,
Nuts and acorns line up for the fun on the line.

Flowers have secrets they whisper with glee,
Telling the breeze, 'You can't catch me!'
Nature's a carnival, laughter rings true,
With each silly moment, joy just renews!

Glowing Green Whispers of Joy

In the heart of the woods, where the shadows play,
A mole made a hat from grass he found stray.
He wears it with pride, looking quite dapper,
As the frogs break into a song, loud and clapper!

Butterflies tell stories of each flower's plight,
While snails hold a race but just chill out and write.
The ferns, they gossip, waving their fronds,
'Who knew muck could be so loved and absconded?'

A chipmunk is juggling acorns with flair,
While the trees cheer him on, with rustles of air.
The sun winks down on this hilarious sight,
And a raincloud scoffs, 'I'll bring in the night!'

But no one is bothered, they're having a blast,
Creating sweet moments that can't be surpassed.
So here's to the laughter where green veggies roam,
In a world full of joy, this nature feels like home!

Luminescent Dews on Forest Floors

Dew drops giggle on morning grass,
They tickle toes as critters pass.
Bouncing bugs wear hats of green,
Their dance a sight, a whimsical scene.

A worm just slipped, and now it's stuck,
"Hey, I was chillin', guess I'm out of luck!"
The mushrooms chuckle, oh what a show,
In this vibrant land, the humor can grow.

The pine trees gossip with leafy glee,
"Did you see that squirrel? Fancy-free!"
The flowers bloom in laughter's name,
While shadows shift, it's all a game.

A snail in shades, feeling so cool,
"Slow down, folks — I'm no racing fool!"
With nature's jokes, this world unfolds,
In giggly corners, life never gets old.

Glistening Auras of Ancient Paths

On a winding trail, where shadows play,
A hedgehog struts like it's a parade.
With gleaming spines, he's quite a sight,
"Oh, do you see me? I'm feeling bright!"

A rabbit hops in a woolly vest,
"Is that a fashion? Well, I must confess!
I've got the look, I'm dressed to thrill,
But soon I'll dash, as fast as a drill!"

The owls are laughing, hooting with cheer,
"Who's the wise guy? We've no reason to fear!"
Amid the ferns, they'll spin a yarn,
Of the greatest chase since the birth of dawn.

A butterfly flits with dainty flair,
"Catch me if you can, if you dare!"
While dragonflies giggle, a sonnet they sing,
In nature's madness, oh what joy they bring.

Whispers of Green Light

In a world where whispers flutter and spin,
The leaves are gabbing, it's quite the din.
"Did you hear that? Oh my, you must—
That critter just wore a tail of rust!"

The grass tickles toes, they squeal and laugh,
Among the rocks, they take a gaff.
A toad croaks, "What a silly show,
I didn't sign up for this, you know!"

Sprinkled light dances over the vale,
Chasing shadows as they begin to flail.
A chipmunk rides on a tiny bike,
Squeaking, "Watch out! I'm ready to strike!"

The air is alive with glee and cheer,
When nature's crew gathers here to steer.
Their playful antics fill the day,
In this world of chuckles, they prance and play.

Emerald Shadows Dance

In emerald realms where shadows prance,
A weary ant tries his luck at dance.
With tiny legs, he takes a leap,
"Oh dear me! Is this too steep?"

A bear nearby says, "That's quite absurd!
Your moves are funny, you're truly heard!"
As the sunlight flickers, a show unfolds,
A party bustles with stories retold.

The ferns sway gently, a rhythmic wave,
A beetle in shades, mighty and brave.
"Let's throw a bash, with giggles galore!
I've brought the snacks, who could want more?"

With bated breath, the crowd begins,
They laugh and tumble, everyone grins.
In this leafy den of joy and chance,
Nature's creatures find their dance.

The Soft Glimmer of Hidden Nature

In shadows green with giggles bright,
A dance of leaves in morning light.
They wiggle and they sway with glee,
Whispering secrets, wild and free.

A critter darts, a squirrel in flight,
Wearing a leaf, oh what a sight!
Laughter echoes through the glade,
Nature's jesters at their trade.

The drops of dew like diamonds flash,
A happy puddle, then a splash!
Frogs croak jokes from their leafy seats,
While ants hold parties with tiny sweets.

With every rustle, a joke unfolds,
In harmony, the forest holds.
Under branches, both wide and tall,
The humor of nature enchants us all.

Forest Whispers at Day's First Glow

Awake, dear woods! Let's crack a grin,
The trees have stories locked within.
With sunbeams tickling each leafy ear,
Whispers of laughter, nature's cheer.

The owls whooped, in tuxedos dressed,
Even the mushrooms are well-expressed.
"Who needs a beard?" a squirrel did jest,
As he scurried past the forest's best.

A rabbit hops on a path quite bold,
Telling tall tales that never grow old.
As needles chuckle, the branches sway,
These woodland friends know how to play.

So listen close, as daylight breaks,
With every chirp, a giggle wakes.
Where nature's humor sprouts, we find,
The frolicsome life of every kind.

Ferns in the Glorious Embrace of Dawn

At dawn, the ferns stretch with grace,
Their fidgeting fronds in a lively race.
Tickled by sunlight, they can't stay still,
Twirling around like a leafy thrill.

A chubby bug joins the dance, how grand!
Waddling along, he shows his hand.
"Step aside, folks, I'm here for the show!"
But trip on a leaf and he faces woe.

The morning dew drips from tipped ends,
A playful splash that nature sends.
Frogs join in with a croaky chime,
As laughter echoes, keeping time.

So frolic forth, oh green brigade,
In this sunny ballet, never fade.
With each bright moment, we share a laugh,
In this glorious world, we find our path.

The Resilience of Light and Leaf

In the forest where shadows play,
Bright spirits rise at the break of day.
Leaves twitch with joy, oh so spry,
Like they've caffeinated, oh me, oh my!

A wise old tree shares tales of yore,
With branches waving, they all adore.
"Life's a breeze with a bit of flair,
Just shake a leg, if you dare!"

Beneath the canopy, fungi stroll,
In funky hats, they make the whole.
Giggles hide in mossy nooks,
Nature's gossip spreads through books.

As laughter rings through leaves and light,
In nature's arms, all feels just right.
With every chuckle, life appears,
A joyful dance that calms all fears.

Beneath the Luminous Fronds

Under leafy wigs, we dance and sway,
Lizards join the jig, hip-hip-hooray!
Bouncing bugs all play their drum,
Even the moss goes wiggly-bum!

Twisting vines with a playful glance,
Who knew plants could really prance?
Bees buzz by with a funky beat,
Plant parties are oh-so-sweet!

Roots that tickle and make us squeal,
"Look out! That's not a meal, that's Neil!"
Ferns in tutus, oh what a sight,
Dancing till the fall of night!

With every step, the earth does giggle,
As rabbits join in, hopping and wriggle.
In a world where laughter will unfurl,
A forest party brings a swirl!

A Serenade of Green Light

Amidst the green, a tune doth float,
A frog in a tux, he's quite the quote!
With every pluck, a leaf does cheer,
It seems that nature loves to sneer!

The mushrooms bob in rhythm too,
Dancing while sprouting, oh how they grew!
Sneaky snails groove on their shells,
Playing tunes that the forest tells.

Squirrels wear shades, looking quite cool,
Diving in leaves like a slippery pool.
The sunlight flickers, oh what a tease,
While nature's band plays tunes with ease!

A chorus of critters gives their shout,
Even the shy flowers tiptoe about.
In this grand show, nobody's a foe,
Just laughter and joy in the green glow.

Shadows that Embrace the Bright

In the shade where silliness reigns,
A raccoon in sunglasses entertains!
He juggles acorns, oh what a hoot,
While the shadows join in, goofing to boot.

Bright sunbeams creep through leaves so sly,
Tickling ferns that laugh and cry.
Pinecones giggle as they roll on by,
Guess even they can't help but try!

The patchwork critters play hide and seek,
In woven laughter, they feel unique.
Chasing the light, they dance and leap,
Until the shadows begin to creep.

In the soft glow, friendships bloom wide,
A merry bunch, with hearts open wide.
Each wink and nod is a joyful delight,
In this playful realm where shadows ignite.

Illuminated Petals of the Forest

Petals sparkle like a prankster's grin,
A butterfly waltzes, inviting a spin!
With every flutter, laughter does rise,
As daisies giggle beneath sunny skies.

A snail on a quest with a shiny shell,
"Watch me slide!", he yells with a swell.
Tickling grass as it sways by chance,
Even the thorns join in for a dance!

Bright blooms joke, they're all in the game,
Their laughs echo loudly, oh what a claim!
Crickets chirp with their own silly cheer,
As the forest rejoices in sunshine near.

Petals of laughter, leaves of delight,
Together they sparkle in colorful light.
A festival blooms with each giggling sound,
In whimsical woods, where fun does abound!

Splendor Under the Verdant Arch

Beneath the leafy cover, oh what a sight,
The plants are mingling, oh what a fright!
A squirrel in a tux, he twirls with glee,
While mushrooms giggle in a leafy spree.

The ferns are whispering secrets at night,
Through vines they're sneaking, such a delight!
A busy bumblebee, dressed up in stripes,
Bumbles right in, catching all the gripes.

Down by the pond, a frog takes a leap,
In a style so grand, he disturbs the sheep.
With dainty footwork, he dances a jig,
While ferns laugh softly, "Oh my, how big!"

So let's raise a toast to this quirky batch,
Where nature's own jesters all make a match!
With each little chuckle, we join the fun,
In a kingdom of green, where life is a pun.

Streams of Light on Ferny Paths

There's a path where the sunlight slips and slides,
Where dandelions laugh and the mischief hides.
A snail in a race, oh what a surprise,
With a shell so grand, he's the crown of the prize.

Ferns throw a party, clad in bright green,
While shadows play tag with the earth in between.
A rabbit shows off his starry-eyed flair,
As he hops through the bushes, oh, what a pair!

A lizard in shades and a crumpled hat,
He struts with a swagger, just like a cat.
The paths are alive with the giggles and grins,
Where the dance of the creatures forever begins.

So roam through this land where the laughter is free,
And join in the antics so wild and so silly.
With every soft rustle and every bright smile,
The light on the ferns makes it all worthwhile.

The Unseen Glow of Wilderness

In the wild where the shadows blend with the light,
Ferns frolic and flirt, oh what a bright sight!
A critter in sunglasses, with flair so divine,
He struts through the grasses, feeling quite fine.

The beetles are buzzing, hosting a show,
With tiny bright lights, they dance to and fro.
A chipmunk in trouble, with crumbs on his chin,
Cracks jokes with the mushrooms, let the fun begin!

Each thicket's a riddle, each whisper a jest,
The brook giggles softly, 'You'll never guess!'
The leaves are all chuckling, just being themselves,
While the entire forest plays up on the shelves.

So if you should wander, take heed of the cheer,
For the unseen glow is what draws us all near.
In a world full of laughter, where spirits take flight,
The wilderness winks, saying, "Join in the light!"

Illuminated Dreams Under Canopies

Under canopies bright, where the dreamers all roam,
Ferns share their secrets, making this place home.
A hedgehog in slippers, he serves up a treat,
While fireflies giggle and tap their small feet.

The shadows are dancing, the smiles abound,
A chorus of chuckles, a joyful sound.
A cat with a hat, perched high on a log,
Whispers to ferns, "I'm the king of the fog!"

Each twist of the branches holds magic untold,
In the heart of this forest, where fun is the gold.
As laughter erupts in this whimsical realm,
The ferns sway and wiggle, joy's at the helm.

So gather your dreams and let laughter prevail,
With each leafy giggle, let nothing curtail.
In the warmth of the light, where the spirits convene,
Under bright leafy rooftops, we reign like a queen!

Tiers of Green in the Quiet Sun

In a corner of the yard, they twirl,
Those sprightly leaves in a little swirl.
They giggle at the squirrels' mad race,
While grasshoppers dance with such grace.

A sneaky snail takes a quick peek,
Feeling proud in its slow little streak.
The sun's high up, not a cloud in sight,
Yet all the bugs play hide and seek, what a delight!

Bumblebees buzzing with quite the flair,
Demanding attention, they don't seem to care.
"Look at us! We're the life of the party!"
Yet none of them ever seem to be tardy!

In the midst of laughter, a worm did creep,
"Why so serious?" it offered a peep.
With laughter and greens, the day was bright,
In their jolly place, everything felt right.

Crafting Light Amongst Leaves

With tiny fingers, they reach for the sun,
Painted in fun, oh what a run!
They tickle the air with their flirty moves,
While the tall shadows sway, just trying to groove.

A froggy friend hops right in,
Joining the dance, with a toothy grin.
"Where's the party?" it croaks with glee,
A jolly ol' bash, come along, you'll see!

In the playful light, ants march and shout,
They turn a small crumb into a large clout.
"Onward to victory!" they chant with pride,
As they haul their treasure, just side by side.

Then comes a breeze, with a tickle and tease,
Making leaves giggle, fluttering with ease.
Underneath the laughter, a secret so dear,
Lies in the light, the fun is right here!

Nature's Quiet Illuminations

Tiny sprouts in a sunny nook,
Whispering secrets, come take a look!
A bumblebee trips on a honey drape,
"Honey, is that you?" it jokes with great shape.

A ladybug with dots, ever the star,
"Do my spots make me pretty from afar?"
The leaves just giggle in the gentle breeze,
"More dots, more fun!" they tease with ease.

A curious chipmunk climbs up a log,
Spying on critters, and the occasional dog.
"Why don't you join us?" the twigs start to call,
"Life here is brighter than at the mall!"

As the day winds down and shadows begin,
Each critter reflects on the day full of spin.
With laughs and with glee, they settle in tight,
Underneath leafy glow, all feels just right.

Shades of Olive Under Rays

Under rock and leaf, the jests do grow,
Twirling in shades of a deep green glow.
A critter parade, all ready to play,
Retelling the tales of a bright sunny day.

Beetles above, performing a show,
With fancy flips, they steal the whole flow.
"Watch me sparkle!" says one with a wink,
"While the world blinks, I'll make them think!"

A wandering fly, quite proud, flits fast,
"Did you see that? I'm a shadowy cast!"
But the leaves just chuckle, too green to fret,
"Your flight's quite a sight, but don't place a bet!"

As twilight whispers its gentle goodnight,
The laughter echoes through the fading light.
In a world full of greens, giggles embrace,
Where every little leaf wears a happy face.

A Symphony of Lushness

In the forest where the dew prances,
Ferns wave like silly dancers.
A laugh erupts from a squirrel nearby,
Is he mocking the trees that sigh?

The leaves giggle under the sun,
Playing hide and seek, just for fun.
With a wiggle and jig, they flutter about,
Shouting secrets that make us shout!

There's a mossy carpet, thick and green,
Where the bunnies hop, a quirky scene.
They're twirling 'round as if in a race,
Do you think they've found the best hiding place?

The breezes whistle a humorous tune,
Tickling the ferns in their leafy cocoon.
A party of shadows under the leaves,
Telling jokes that no one believes!

Shadows of Ancient Growths

In the stillness of the dusky glades,
Ferns play tricks in leafy cascades.
With a rustle and shake, they tease the deer,
"Come dance with us! We won't disappear!"

Old trunks creak, telling tales of yore,
As critters gather—a feathery chore.
Though covered in fluff, they strut with pride,
What a sight to see, nature's own ride!

The ferns whisper jokes to the starry skies,
"Oh look! There's a raccoon with big brown eyes!"
They snicker as owls hoot their fat puns,
The whole forest giggles, oh what fun!

Even the shadows can't keep a straight face,
As the moon joins in this leafy embrace.
In the depths where ancient tales grow,
Life's a jest, and we're all in the show!

Green Halos in the Woods

Cloaked in emeralds, the ferns do sway,
Inviting all creatures to join their play.
"Stop in the circle, don't hide behind,
We've got stories of the best kind!"

The fronds are tiptoeing, looking quite spry,
Creating a ruckus as they flutter and fly.
"Come chase the sunbeams, don't be a bore,
There's plenty of fun and so much to explore!"

Beneath an archway of leafy delight,
Even the mushrooms can't help but delight.
"What's green, has leaves, and loves to boast?
It's us, the ferns, starring in our own post!"

Laughter echoes through roots intertwined,
As the woodland revelers unwind.
With each swish and sway, they throw a grand ball,
Where nature herself is the life of it all!

Portrait of a Serene Oasis

In a tranquil nook where the greenery sighs,
Ferns unfold secrets under the skies.
With arms stretched wide, they softly implore,
"Leave your troubles, there's fun at the door!"

A frog on a lily leaps like it's grand,
Poking fun at the trees with a wave of its hand.
The ferns chuckle, "What a silly sight!
Join our party, it feels just right!"

The sunlight dances on dew-kissed leaves,
Sharing tales only the forest believes.
As the breeze carries laughter, light and free,
A portrait of joy—a spiraled jubilee.

Every twist of the frond speaks of leisure,
Crafting whimsical moments beyond all measure.
With each gentle sway, nature's delight,
A serene oasis buzzing with light!

Whispers of the Verdant Glow

In the shade, ferns gently confide,
Chattering leaves, oh what a ride!
They giggle and wiggle under the light,
A verdant dance, what a silly sight!

Their fronds wave high, like they just won the game,
Tickled by breezes, they never feel tame.
With each little rustle, they send out a cheer,
"Come join us, humans, stop sweating in fear!"

Lying down beneath their leafy parade,
I swear I heard one say, "Look, I made a shade!"
They plot and they prance, those green little jesters,
With laughter that ripples, they're nature's best testers!

Between the tall trees, they sway and they tease,
With secrets they share as they shimmy in breeze.
A comedy show, right there on the ground,
Where nature's own jesters are joyously found!

Radiance Among the Leaves

In the thicket where the veggies would frown,
Ferns stretch upwards, donning green crowns.
"The sun's got a crush!" one frond teased away,
While another laughed out, "What a bright display!"

They prank all the pigeons, who strut like they own,
Pretending to twirl, in their leafy green zone.
"Dance for us, ferns!" demanded a bug,
But they just rolled over, giving him a shrug!

A squirrel nearby chuckled, "What's so grand?"
"Life in our shade is simply unplanned!"
The ferns threw a party, all petals and cheer,
With whispers of laughter that all friends could hear!

In the green spotlight, their antics abound,
Creating delights that can't be unwound.
"Oh look!" said a leaf, "Here comes my twin!
Should we both dance, or just one of us win?"

Emerald Dancers in Warmth

Fern friends in formation, doing their groove,
Beneath glowing rays, they find their smooth move.
"Yo, check my flourish!" a frond exclaimed,
While others cut in, "You're just a little famed!"

With jigs and with hops from the warm mossy floor,
They giggle and wiggle, who could ask for more?
One fern said, "Lighten up, why so uptight?"
While gleeful leaves shimmered, "Let's dance through the night!"

Behind them, a toad croaked, "You're stealing my shine!"

The ferns just threw back, "Oh, we're yours in time!"
"Come join our merry, it's wacky and bright,
Let's boogie together till the end of the night!"

So under the glimmer of playful daylight,
Emerald dancers filled the world with delight.
With every sway and a slow flirtatious bend,
They spread laughter and mixed joy without end!

The Glistening Canopy

Ferns looked up, and they couldn't complain,
"Could we get any bolder, let's riot for rain!"
They spritzed on each other, like a raucous parade,
And giggled as droplets made their own cascade!

"Sprinkle us lightly, oh heavenly mist,
We'll take a quick dip, can't let this chance twist!"
They played peek-a-boo with the tall, swaying trees,
"Tag! You're it, buddy!" came through with a breeze!

As shadows danced joyfully across the terrain,
The ferns threw a fiesta, in wild, gleeful strain.
"Oh, look at us shine, aren't we quite the crew?"
"I'm not sure about you; I'm feeling quite dew!"

So under the canvas of bright, dappled glee,
The ferns staged a riot, just wild as can be.
With laughter and joy, they lit up the glade,
While woodland friends wondered, "What mischief they've made!"

www.ingramcontent.com/pod-product-compliance
Lightning Source LLC
Chambersburg PA
CBHW070322120526
44590CB00017B/2780